D1526161

PRESENCE

AN ADVENT DEVOTIONAL

Dwell

AN ADVENT DEVOTIONAL

PRESENCE

PRESENCE: AN ADVENT DEVOTIONAL

Contents

[11]You make known to me the path of life; in YOUR PRESENCE there is fullness of joy; at your right hand are pleasures forevermore.

PSALM 16:11

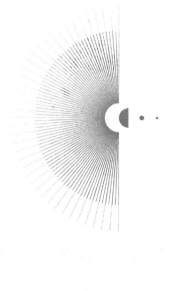

Introduction

"God is not ashamed of the lowliness of human beings. God marches right in. He chooses people as his instruments and performs his wonders WHERE ONE WOULD LEAST EXPECT THEM. God is near to lowliness; he loves the lost, the neglected, the unseemly, the excluded, the weak and broken."

DIETRICH BONHOEFFER

WE ARE NEAR TO THE PLACES AND PEOPLE we love. We do not love the idea of a favorite coffee shop. We love the smell of freshly brewed coffee and the taste on our tongues. We may love the romance of the English countryside or the Italian coast, yet daydreaming about an exotic place is a far cry from a day immersed in exploring medieval towns and coastal villages. Similarly, our love for people requires proximity, entering their joys and sorrows as we share life together.

If to love is to will the good of another, as it has often been said, then it is impossible to love at a distance. Only in intimate community do we learn the needs of another and know how to act for their good. We offer love as we come to know the object of our love, and we receive love as we open our hearts to another, believing our deepest hopes and fears are held with great care and respect.

Advent is the glorious celebration of God's nearness to those he loves. Though we are weak and weary from the sickness of sin, our Lord does not despise our lowliness. Instead, he dignifies our humanity with the gift of his presence. He loves us at our worst and proves that love to be true by taking our very life upon himself, entering our death so that we might know his life.

In the following pages, you will find daily reflections on the wonder of God's presence with us in Jesus. And yet, here at the start, a question is posed to each of us: are we present to God? As he is near to us in Christ, are we moving toward him in love, or do we love at a distance? God is with us. Over the coming weeks, we must daily ask ourselves, "Are we with God?"

"And he made from one man every nation of mankind to live on all the face of the earth, having determined allotted periods and the boundaries of their dwelling place, that they should seek God, and perhaps feel their way toward him and find him. Yet he is actually not far from each one of us, for 'In him we live and move and have our being.'" Acts 17:26-28a

FIRST
WEEK

¹I was glad when
they said to me,
"LET US GO to the
house of the Lord!"

PSALM 122:1

of Advent

SUNDAY

Walk in the Light

 OPEN DWELL AND LISTEN TO

Isaiah 2:1-5; Psalm 122; Romans 13:11-14; Matthew 24:36-44

"Trust that the Lord is always a provider for those who take refuge in Him."

ST. MACARIUS THE GREAT

"WALK IN THE LIGHT." Here we encounter a common biblical exhortation found throughout the pages of Scripture. These words have immediate traction and relevance in our culture. Walk in the light and avoid darkness. Seems simple enough, right? And yet the challenge before us is the seemingly elusive nature of light, how it often dances in the shadows and evades our sight.

We know we are meant to walk in the light, yet our hearts and minds struggle to discern the true light that gives light to all.

In fact, our world is awash with beliefs and values that *claim* to be light yet, in reality, lead us in the way of darkness and decay. Simply put, the human heart longs for the way of light, yet requires divine illumination to know the way it must go. We long for God, to know him and to be known by him, yet sin has distorted our desires and twisted our understanding of the straight and narrow. Therefore, before we set out on a journey, we must be sure it is, in fact, the Light of God toward which we move!

For this reason, Isaiah invites the house of Jacob to "walk in the light *of the LORD* (Isa 2:5). Our eyes must be trained to see the light of God as the one true source of life, the way from which we must never depart. And in the goodness and mercy of God, as the season of Advent reminds us, the light of the LORD is not an abstract belief or set of philosophical positions but the presence of a person: Jesus Christ, God With Us. In his embodied and incarnate self, he is the light of God, or as he says, "the way, and the truth, and the life" (John 14:6).

Prayer for the Week

Almighty God, give us grace to cast away the works of darkness, and put on the armor of light, now in the time of this mortal life in which your Son Jesus Christ came to visit us in great humility; that in the last day, when he shall come again in his glorious majesty to judge both the living and the dead, we may rise to the life immortal; through him who lives and reigns with you and the Holy Spirit, one God, now and for ever. *Amen.*

Reflective Practice

Are there ways in which you have abstracted truth or separated the "light of the LORD" from the presence and person of Jesus Christ?

MONDAY

Remember Your People

 OPEN DWELL AND LISTEN TO
Psalm 124; Genesis 8:1-19; Romans 6:1-11

"We ought to remember God even more often than we breathe."

ST. GREGORY NAZIANZEN

REMEMBRANCE. A WORD THAT CAN INSTANTLY conjure both nostalgic joy and deep pain. To remember is, in some sense, to carry the past with you in the present. It is naive to think we look backward with fully detached and unaffected hearts, as though past experiences are disconnected from the lived reality of this very moment. Rather, memory as a *living* connection with our past is central to our identity as human beings.

In Scripture, the act of remembrance is central to the story of salvation. As important as it is for us to remember the moments of joy and pain that have shaped our lives, the true act of remembrance on which our very existence depends is *God's* memory of us. Again, this is not a simple acknowledgment of existence or warm feelings toward someone. For God to remember his people is to sustain, protect, and draw them into the very story of creation.

As we see in today's reading, "God remembered Noah and all the beasts and all the livestock that were with him in the ark" (Gen 8:1). God's remembrance is dynamic, leading to the preservation of creation, redeeming it from the evils that sought to bring it down. In this way, the story of the ark is a forerunner of the story of Advent, for it is in the birth of Christ that we see God once again remembering his people, drawing near in the flesh to remember and make whole those he loves.

Prayer for the Week

Almighty God, give us grace to cast away the works of darkness, and put on the armor of light, now in the time of this mortal life in which your Son Jesus Christ came to visit us in great humility; that in the last day, when he shall come again in his glorious majesty to judge both the living and the dead, we may rise to the life immortal; through him who lives and reigns with you and the Holy Spirit, one God, now and for ever. *Amen.*

Reflective Practice

In what ways does the ancient story of God drawing near in Christ directly shape and impact your life today?

TUESDAY

On Our Side

 OPEN DWELL AND LISTEN TO

Psalm 124; Genesis 9:1-17; Hebrews 11:32-40

"He who gives you the day will also give you the things necessary for the day."

ST. GREGORY OF NYSSA

YOUR UNDERSTANDING OF SOMEONE'S character directly impacts the nature of your relationship with that person. If you believe them to be trustworthy, you are more inclined to vulnerably open your heart and life to them, believing they will neither exploit nor abuse your trust. Conversely, if someone has given you a reason to be suspicious of their motives or actions, you will do all you can to distance yourself and those you love.

While this is true of every human relationship, it is all the more true of our life with God. When you think of God, what type of being do you envision? In your heart of hearts, do you believe him to be good, trustworthy, and kind, or do you see him as distant and ineffective, unconcerned with the cares of your heart or the needs of your community? Taken a step further, perhaps it isn't simply God as an absentee father, but God as an evil and cruel dictator, unmoved and unaffected by the suffering you have experienced.

Psalm 124 reminds us of a profound truth at the very heart of the Scriptural narrative: *God is on our side* (Ps 124:1).

He is for you, loves you more than you love yourself, and longs to see you flourish in this life and the next. And this is not only God's promise to you, but is the hope of the entire world. How do we know this to be true? Because, in the birth of Christ, we see that God is not only on our side but also *at our side*. He so deeply identifies with his creation that he refuses to cheer it on from a distance. Instead, he enters the raging chaos to walk with us and lead us into places of peace.

Prayer for the Week

Almighty God, give us grace to cast away the works of darkness, and put on the armor of light, now in the time of this mortal life in which your Son Jesus Christ came to visit us in great humility; that in the last day, when he shall come again in his glorious majesty to judge both the living and the dead, we may rise to the life immortal; through him who lives and reigns with you and the Holy Spirit, one God, now and for ever. *Amen.*

Reflective Practice

Who do you believe God to be? To what degree does your honest answer to this question align with the description of God's character in Psalm 124?

WEDNESDAY

A Complete Picture

 OPEN DWELL AND LISTEN TO
Psalm 124; Isaiah 54:1-10; Matthew 24:23-35

*"If there were no tribulation, there would be no rest; if there were
no winter, there would be no summer."*

ST. JOHN CHRYSOSTOM

MATTHEW 24, ALONG WITH THE BOOK OF REVELATION and the
second half of Daniel, are parts of the Bible that rarely make it into
a child's Sunday school lesson. We fear these apocalyptic images of
God will confuse or even contradict the "meek and mild" vision of the
Good Shepherd that we long to instill in our little ones. In all honesty,
the same tension exists for Christians of any age. How can we make
sense of these seemingly contradictory pictures of God and his
relationship to the world?

When we write off entire portions of Scripture or dismiss them as
inconvenient or simply too confusing to be helpful, we risk accepting
an incomplete picture of God and his work in our world. We cling to
the humility and warmth of the babe in the manger yet fail to see how
this same babe is the one who will come again "with power and great
glory," sending out his angels to bring justice and judgment to the
earth (Matt 24:30-31).

In Advent, we are explicitly invited to hold these two visions of
Christ close together in our hearts and minds. Just as the humility
of the first Advent is for our good, so too is the promised Second
Advent, the return of Christ in glory, to be celebrated by the faithful

as a continuation of God's healing presence in the world. The same babe that vulnerably entered the chaos of creation now sits above it, commanding the sun and moon, wind and waves, and every human power on earth, speaking justice and bringing peace to every corner of his creation.

Prayer for the Week

Almighty God, give us grace to cast away the works of darkness, and put on the armor of light, now in the time of this mortal life in which your Son Jesus Christ came to visit us in great humility; that in the last day, when he shall come again in his glorious majesty to judge both the living and the dead, we may rise to the life immortal; through him who lives and reigns with you and the Holy Spirit, one God, now and for ever. *Amen.*

Reflective Practice

Christians have always received seasons of preparation, such as Advent or Lent, as invitations into a life of repentance. As you prepare for the birth of Christ and look ahead to his return in glory, what steps can you take to grow in a commitment to humility and repentance as a way of life?

THURSDAY

Impossible Dreams

 OPEN DWELL AND LISTEN TO

Psalm 72:1-7, 18-19; Isaiah 4:2-6; Acts 1:12-17, 21-26

"We must live as if in the heavenly kingdom, dwelling there in
anticipation by hope."

ST. JOHN OF KRONSTADT

LET THE KING BE SO WISE THAT HE CAN *know God's decisions and*
show God's character! And let him live as long as the moon! People
centuries ago certainly knew that people don't live as long as the
moon. But how else could they express their hope in such a beautiful
dream?

Sometimes, in moments of great longing, we say more than we mean
and come to a deeper truth. In a no-holds-barred request, the psalmist
in today's passage asks for a perfect human expression of God's
leadership. Imagine it—lasting as long as the moon: no changing
regimes, no coups, no shifting (or shifty) agendas, but a perfect king
with a peaceful reign that will allow not just the individual but the
community—society itself—to rest secure.

And what does this dream look like? The psalmist sees a flourishing
hill country, a functional government. Isaiah sees prize-winning
produce, a bustling city, a beautiful outdoor canopy where people can
gather and rest. Acts even tastes this vision: decision-makers relying
on God and agreeing together—without a single fight!

In the hope of God's justice, his people long for a flourishing natural world, good social systems, and governance based on caring for the poor and needy rather than self-preservation. This kingdom, the psalmist sings, will be a refreshment—as refreshing as cool rain on newly mown grass. This stands opposed to what's *not* refreshing— anything that feels like the "same old, same old" power grabs and neglect of the weak.

Is this healed society only a spiritual one? It doesn't seem like the psalmist thinks so. Is it impossible? A utopian dream? If we're dreaming alone, it certainly is. But Scripture seems to think God dreams with us, "who alone does wondrous things" (Ps 72:18). How dare we hope for such a king, such a kingdom, unless He Who is Able is behind that hope?

Prayer for the Week

Almighty God, give us grace to cast away the works of darkness, and put on the armor of light, now in the time of this mortal life in which your Son Jesus Christ came to visit us in great humility; that in the last day, when he shall come again in his glorious majesty to judge both the living and the dead, we may rise to the life immortal; through him who lives and reigns with you and the Holy Spirit, one God, now and for ever. *Amen.*

Reflective Practice

What good thing in this world seems too big to hope for? Sketch it on paper in images or words (for example, higher wages, equitable healthcare, honest politics, end to pollution, healing of a loved one—anything). Look at your vision. God's vision is even greater. Boldly pray for one impossible thing today.

FRIDAY

Vulnerable

 OPEN DWELL AND LISTEN TO
Psalm 72:1-7, 18-19; Isaiah 30:19-26; Acts 13:16-25

"What does it cost us to say: 'My God help me! Have mercy on me!'
Is there anything easier than this? And this little will suffice to
save us if we be diligent in doing it."

ST. ALPHONSUS LIGUORI

YOU'D BE HARD-PRESSED TO FIND THIS passage in Scripture:
"God rushes to the strong...He bends to the cry of the victorious...He
stoops down to the least needy among them...He is near to the A-OK."
Of course, we don't have to fail or be at the end of our rope for God
to be near us. Neither do we need to be wounded, depressed, afraid,
or afflicted for the Lord to want to be with us. He is also the God of
happiness, laughter, festivity, and simple contentment.

And yet the greatest promises of Scripture do seem exactly for those
at their lowest: for those who are weeping, graciousness (Isa 30:19);
for the unsure, confidence and direction (v 21); for those enslaved to
image and idols, freedom (v 22); for the hungry, food (v 23), for the
dry, water (v 25); for those in a dark place, light (v 26). And to those in
adversity and affliction, he offers the sight of his face (v 20).

In Acts, St. Paul describes God's patient dealings with his people and
then calls Jesus Israel's "savior." No matter what place we happen
to be personally—how well-behaved our kids, how comfortable our
paychecks, how satisfied with life and work—the story of God coming
to his people since the Fall has always been a rescue op. At times

it is urgent, at times slow and gentle, but always ongoing until it's complete.

If cries and tears get God's attention—even when the suffering is our fault—then let's be quick to be vulnerable before God. It is no use hiding and no good acting as if we don't need to be saved. The faster we cry out for help, the faster he comes to our aid, whatever help we need.

Prayer for the Week

Almighty God, give us grace to cast away the works of darkness, and put on the armor of light, now in the time of this mortal life in which your Son Jesus Christ came to visit us in great humility; that in the last day, when he shall come again in his glorious majesty to judge both the living and the dead, we may rise to the life immortal; through him who lives and reigns with you and the Holy Spirit, one God, now and for ever. *Amen.*

Reflective Practice

If you are in a place of joy or contentment today, take a moment to breathe, be still, and give thanks. If you are not, or know someone who is not, take a moment to breathe, be still, and sit in silence. Sit shiva with (stay still with the grief of) your trouble for at least seven minutes without asking, solving, or excusing. Try doing this with your hand on your heart.

SATURDAY

God's Road

 OPEN DWELL AND LISTEN TO

Psalm 72:1-7, 18-19; Isaiah 40:1-11; John 1:19-28

---

*"Humanity's final goal: communion with God. The path to it: faith
and walking in the commandments with the aid of divine grace....
Here is the path—start walking!"*

ST. THEOPHAN THE RECLUSE

IF YOU'VE EVER BUSHWHACKED in the woods or know what it's like
to cross a desert, you know making "a way in the wilderness" is not easy.

What kind of road is a wilderness way? It is first a road "for our
God"—divine access to every part of the earth. It is his royal road.
God will show up, and there's no corner of our world he won't show
up in, no matter how unlikely or remote. But it's also our "limited
mobility access" to wherever God will go. God commands that even
the mountains and valleys, the rocky terrain, the wild extremities,
the complex and forbidding, be made straight and smooth. *We* need a
ramp, a clear path, to walk this royal road.

When we think of the things humans hope for most deeply—namely, a
good life with God—this divine proclamation of God's road flies in the
face of our objections:

I'll never see this happen. It's too complicated. Too hard.

*Only the special people will ever get there. I'm too average. Too busy. Not
spiritual enough.*

But this is not true. We hear, "All people are like grass," and we see a Good Shepherd walking along, leading his sheep. In this life, we are all like fragile grass, dependent sheep, helpless lambs, ewes so heavy with young that, ever at our most fruitful, we can only go slowly. We need God's power to step onto his awesome road. And we need much gentleness and help to walk it.

The "way of the Lord" is God's road through our country and our road to God's country. When he makes it plain, will we be humble enough to step up? To keep walking? Will we be willing to help others, too?

Prayer for the Week

Almighty God, give us grace to cast away the works of darkness, and put on the armor of light, now in the time of this mortal life in which your Son Jesus Christ came to visit us in great humility; that in the last day, when he shall come again in his glorious majesty to judge both the living and the dead, we may rise to the life immortal; through him who lives and reigns with you and the Holy Spirit, one God, now and for ever. *Amen.*

Reflective Practice

Listen to a recording of Handel's *Messiah* (perhaps while you're cooking, cleaning, or commuting) or find a live concert to attend. If you have limited time, focus on one or more of these movements: "Comfort Ye," "Every Valley," and "He Shall Feed His Flock." Listen for the double themes of tenderness and power. Hear the words addressed to you, to your flock.

SECOND
WEEK

———

of Advent

SUNDAY

Hidden Life

 OPEN DWELL AND LISTEN TO
Isaiah 11:1-10; Psalm 72:1-7, 18-19; Romans 15:4-13; Matthew 3:1-12

"In everything, whether it is a thing sensed or a thing known, God himself is hidden within."

ST. BONAVENTURE

STUMPS ARE SURPRISING. THEY OFTEN PRESERVE strong and lively roots, but in secret. The tree survives underground but is not thriving above; it's still holding on, but not freely waving branches to the sun and air. This is something like Israel under Roman occupation just before the birth of Christ. Holding on to the gift of the Law, traditions, and identity but not free, not at liberty to flourish.

Sickness, sin, political dysfunction—tyrannies small and large—keep God's people suppressed. That doesn't mean they don't struggle to be faithful and live good lives. But what about God's promise of a "great nation," of true liberty? Surely there is more. What about the promise to be a blessing to all? The unbroken reign of perfect peace and justice—where is that?

At times in their history, God's people have been so worn down, such a thin shadow of all they are meant to be, that when their prophets see the truth through the veneer of "doing okay," they only see a stump. But they also see the tree. Electric green, small at first, shocking against the gray and brown, a tender curl unfolds against the hardened wood. The new shoot is part of the stump, proof of its profound life, yet it is also something new, unlooked for, a harbinger of the future.

The reign of peace promised by God will begin suddenly, surprisingly, as a little sprig.

What is most promising in God's eyes often begins not with stratagems, careful preservation of what we've known, or holding on with gritted teeth but with tenderness and vulnerability. The shoot of Jesse is the sign of a whole new age of life for God's family tree. This will truly be God's work, and as we see in Isaiah and hear from John, it will reveal God's dearest will for them, for us.

Prayer for the Week

Merciful God, who sent your messengers the prophets to preach repentance and prepare the way for our salvation: Give us grace to heed their warnings and forsake our sins, that we may greet with joy the coming of Jesus Christ our Redeemer; who lives and reigns with you and the Holy Spirit, one God, now and for ever. Amen.

Reflective Practice

Has Jesus ever surprised you? Have you ever asked him to or let him? What would that surprise look like, and how might you search for it? Jot down some ideas. A change in your prayer practice? Visiting a worship tradition you're not familiar with? Seeing how various artists have depicted Jesus? Reading a whole Gospel in one sitting? Bless someone today with a surprise gift, favor, or word. Ask the Lord to surprise you this Advent.

MONDAY

Are You Ready?

 OPEN DWELL AND LISTEN TO
Psalm 21; Isaiah 24:1-16a; 1 Thessalonians 4:1-12

"The fear that makes us turn quickly away from everything that is not good, and with all our heart and mind collapse against our Lord's breast…comes from God's grace. Any fear that does not is either wrong or tainted."

JULIAN OF NORWICH

SOME OF THE BEST GIFTS COME WITH sober warnings. It used to be that if you were a teenager who wanted your driver's license, you had to first watch videos about the dangers of driving and the importance of sobriety, wearing your seatbelt and obeying the speed limit. While the videos could be over-the-top, they were meant to shock teens into carefully appreciating and properly receiving what they were about to be given.

In many wedding services, the bride and groom are admonished before the vows about the serious responsibilities of marriage and warned not to take them lightly. Premarital counseling, family involvement, and all the agonies of decision-making—even the financial investment—all underline the seriousness of a wedding and the greatness of the change that's about to take place.

The best decisions we make don't rely on fear or pressure. But most significant rites of passage look deep in our eyes, so to speak, and ask, *Are you ready?* The coming of the Messiah will be a passage of God's people, the world, and each one of us from one age—one reality—

to another. Isaiah describes the drying up of all wine and music—a moment of total sobriety, joy's "eventide" before the dawn of a new joy, new praise we haven't yet known.

Even St. Paul urges the Thessalonians to live ready for and responsible with the joy that is and is to come, not like people who need scare tactics to stay in line. In simplicity, in good and upright relationships, with clean hands and hearts, we show God we take the glad and sobering tidings of his great gift seriously.

Prayer for the Week

Merciful God, who sent your messengers the prophets to preach repentance and prepare the way for our salvation: Give us grace to heed their warnings and forsake our sins, that we may greet with joy the coming of Jesus Christ our Redeemer; who lives and reigns with you and the Holy Spirit, one God, now and for ever. Amen.

Reflective Practice

Light a candle. Sit or stand. Slow your breathing. In a moment of prayer, reflect on how you typically make decisions. How did you make your last few significant decisions? How often do you rely on fear, guilt, or other pressures? Can you be guided more deeply by joy and holy desire? Ask the Lord to grow you in this area.

TUESDAY

Poetry of Love

 OPEN DWELL AND LISTEN TO
Psalm 21; Isaiah 41:14-20; Romans 15:14-21

"He has created you out of nothing in His own likeness and image. He has delivered you from your slavery, sending down His Only-begotten Son. He protects you, every hour and every moment, from your enemies. He fights your battles. He prepares the body and blood of His beloved Son for your food. All this is a sign of God's great favor and love for you."

ST. NICODEMUS OF THE HOLY MOUNTAIN

CRUSHING ENEMIES, THRESHING MOUNTAINS. Signs and wonders. Tempests and flying arrows. Barren deserts bursting suddenly into diverse biomes and lush oriental gardens. Sometimes in Scripture, metaphors pile up, nearly fall apart, or become borderline absurd under the power of what they're trying to describe.

Today we are on the very edge of what words can convey. We are in the world of poetry. This is perhaps why, in Scripture, so much prophecy is poetry. We're seeing straight into the very works of God. Trying to tell others what you see is like describing a comet as it is coming at you, capturing each note of every instrument in a 200-piece orchestra, or drinking from a waterfall. What looks or sounds like distortion—even violence—is a peek behind the curtain of ancient wisdom, a flash of the lightning of God's love, a new thing shooting up through the middle of the old.

We can barely imagine what God can do, is about to do, to win our peace.

But notice what he doesn't do: replace his beloved people with less troublesome people, ignore prayers because they are imperfect, disregard the thirsty, or leave those without faith to themselves.

Several times in today's verses, this same lightning-bright, wild warrior Lord is the one who "helps." The one who dazzles and dizzies us with a glimpse of his power shares it through stooping, helping, and serving his creatures—especially the neediest, the least served, and the farthest away. This power and this self-giving are not separate parts of God that he activates at different times. They are the character of one and the same Lord, one single movement of everlasting love.

Prayer for the Week

Merciful God, who sent your messengers the prophets to preach repentance and prepare the way for our salvation: Give us grace to heed their warnings and forsake our sins, that we may greet with joy the coming of Jesus Christ our Redeemer; who lives and reigns with you and the Holy Spirit, one God, now and for ever. Amen.

Reflective Practice

Are you more likely to give help or receive it? If you're more of a "giver," ask for help with one thing this Advent—whether you technically need it or not—from baking cookies or trimming the tree to laundry or elder care. If you're more of a "receiver," schedule one to two hours of your time to help or serve someone else.

WEDNESDAY

Earthy Prayer

 OPEN DWELL AND LISTEN TO

Psalm 21; Genesis 15:1-18; Matthew 12:33-37

"Pray, hope, and don't worry. God is merciful and will hear your prayer. Prayer is the key to God's heart."

ST. PADRE PIO

GOD'S PROMISES ARE GRAND. It's not that we humans don't long for rescue from death and evil, for eternity, for the restoration of the whole earth. But we also have hopes and longings that are simpler, more immediate. O Lord God, what will you give me? For I continue childless. Spouseless. Without satisfying work. Renting when I'd rather own. Praying for healing. Lonely. Restless. In need of a challenge. In need of a break. Without a good savings account. Without this one prayer answered. O Lord, what will you give me?

Sometimes with these simpler longings in our hearts, encountering God's greatest gifts can feel like almost too much or even beside the point, like asking for a meal and instead being handed a very successful stock market portfolio. The good news is that the Lord never asks us to hide our immediate, earthly, and "earthy" desires; neither does he leave us there. Notice: Jesus most chastises those who try to disguise their earthly desires and questions as "spiritual" ones, and he most honors those who are honest about what they want, who bring their honest questions to him. He sees in them the seed of the Kingdom.

The Lord is ahead of us—not only one step but each step, drawing each of our heartaches, hopes, and requests into a bigger picture.

God doesn't scorn Abram's sorrow or confusion. Instead, he reminds Abram that he has been faithful; he is being faithful; he will be faithful. And he honors the faith that Abram shows. Not only will God answer Abram's dearest prayers, but the answer, still to come, is already part of a greater covenant, a more amazing birth—though Abram has to take a leap of faith to believe it.

Prayer for the Week

Merciful God, who sent your messengers the prophets to preach repentance and prepare the way for our salvation: Give us grace to heed their warnings and forsake our sins, that we may greet with joy the coming of Jesus Christ our Redeemer; who lives and reigns with you and the Holy Spirit, one God, now and for ever. Amen.

Reflective Practice

Do you have a Nativity scene? See if you can leave the manger empty until Christmas Eve or Day. Write a prayer request, one of your most persistent, on a slip of paper. Place it in the scene. Spend a few moments sharing your request with God, waiting along with Mary and Joseph, the angels, animals, and shepherds. You're not alone. Ask the Lord for his answer and for his peace.

THURSDAY

An Inconvenient Family Tree

 OPEN DWELL AND LISTEN TO
Psalm 146:5-10; Ruth 1:6-18; 2 Peter 3:1-10

"Nowhere other than looking at himself in the mirror of the Cross can man better understand how much he is worth."

ST. ANTHONY OF PADUA

NOWADAYS, THERE ARE MANY WAYS TO trace our genealogies. Taking a deep dive into our histories can be both exciting and scary. While we could find a connection to someone famous, we could also uncover relations we'd just as soon keep hidden. The more we learn about our genealogies, the more we may find we're not who we thought we were.

This is certainly true of Jesus and his genealogy. Through his adoptive father, Joseph, Jesus' lineage is traced back to Abraham in Matthew and even further back to Adam in Luke. It's a daunting list of names, and we are often tempted to skip over it and start with Jesus' birth in a manger in Bethlehem. Yet, Jesus' earthly genealogy sets the stage for his entire earthly ministry, offering key clues into who this Messiah is. Jesus' connection to certain historical individuals forewarns us: the long-anticipated Christ is not exactly what people are expecting.

This is particularly apparent in Matthew's genealogy, which includes five women: Mary, Tamar, Rahab, Bathsheba, and Ruth. With the exception of his mother, the other four women could be considered embarrassing familial connections for Jesus. Tamar lied and seduced her father-in-law. Rahab was a prostitute. Bathsheba isn't even mentioned by name but is referred to as the wife of Uriah, calling attention to King David's guilt in Uriah's death. Finally, there's Ruth, a good and loyal daughter-in-law to Naomi who is, nevertheless, a Moabite—whom Jews were prohibited from marrying under the Law of Moses. Amazingly, these are exactly the relatives we should expect Jesus to claim. Jesus came to save sinners: not only among the Jewish people but also among all nations. Jesus' genealogy is a great comfort: in our baptism, Jesus also claims us, sinners of every nation under the sun, as his brothers and sisters. This relation, above all others, tells us who we are and whose we are.

Prayer for the Week

Merciful God, who sent your messengers the prophets to preach repentance and prepare the way for our salvation: Give us grace to heed their warnings and forsake our sins, that we may greet with joy the coming of Jesus Christ our Redeemer; who lives and reigns with you and the Holy Spirit, one God, now and for ever. Amen.

Reflective Practice

Consider a difficult relationship in your life. How has this person's behavior or personality pushed you out of his or her life and made that person extremely difficult to love? Now consider how your own behavior and personality push Jesus out of your life and make you extremely difficult to love. Pray for the humility to reconcile with Jesus as you pray for the wisdom to learn to better love the difficult person in your life. Just as Jesus claims the most inconvenient among us as brother or sister, we should learn to do the same.

FRIDAY

Wake-up Call

 OPEN DWELL AND LISTEN TO

Psalm 146:5-10; Ruth 4:13-17; 2 Peter 3:11-18

"While the world changes, the cross stands firm."

ST. BRUNO

WE OFTEN THINK OF PEACE AS PASSIVE. We may think of a beach, staring out at a beautiful sunset, the ocean waves lapping at our feet. We also think of peace as a blank space. It is what remains when war and violence have been removed. It is also that other hazy place where we imagine our dead. We want their souls to rest in peace. Though there is certainly a place for these hazy, abstract definitions of peace, they can lull us away from the more active call that the Prince of Peace issues to us.

We can see this in 2 Peter, where the vehemence of the language jolts us out of sleepy complacency the way a rooster rouses us from sleep. St. Peter knows a thing or two about wake-up calls. During our Lord's passion, when the going got tough, St. Peter got carried away by the pressure of the crowd and denied Jesus three times. He was awakened to his cowardly complacency by a rooster's crow. Now he is *our* rooster, a fellow sinner issuing a call to sinners down through the ages: "Take care that you are not carried away with the error of lawless people and lose your own stability." The subtext could read: "It happened to me. Don't let it happen to you."

As Christians, there is certainly a place for rest, but not for complacency. If we are to take our Sabbath day on the shore of life, we must be sure that the soothing waves do not, in fact, dislodge our feet and pull us under. Even in our rest we must be active, for the tide of public opinion will always seek to carry us further and further out to sea. Before we know it, the firm ground has given way to deep darkness, patiently waiting to swallow us whole. Hear the wake-up call and swim against the current to remain at Jesus' side.

Prayer for the Week

Merciful God, who sent your messengers the prophets to preach repentance and prepare the way for our salvation: Give us grace to heed their warnings and forsake our sins, that we may greet with joy the coming of Jesus Christ our Redeemer; who lives and reigns with you and the Holy Spirit, one God, now and for ever. *Amen.*

Reflective Practice

This evening, when you are most tired, take fifteen minutes to sit upright or stand before going to bed. Read or listen to an account of St. Peter denying Jesus (for instance, in John 18:15-27). Consider a time in your own life when you have bowed to the pressure of the crowd to deny your Christian faith. Consider how God may be issuing a wake-up call to turn back to him. Pray for forgiveness and for the strength to keep your feet when the tide tries to pull you away from the shores of your faith.

SATURDAY

Naughty and Nice

 OPEN DWELL AND LISTEN TO

Psalm 146:5-10; 1 Samuel 2:1-8; Luke 3:1-18

---

*"We hope that the mercy of God may be gained with many
tears and requisite satisfaction on the part of those who have
lapsed. While we live in this body, no one's rehabilitation is to be
despaired of."*

ST. LEO THE GREAT

AT THIS TIME OF YEAR, WE HEAR a good deal about the naughty
and the nice. The nice get presents at Christmas; the naughty get a
lump of coal. There are quite a few passages in Scripture that make it
seem like God has a list for the good and the bad. For instance, Psalm
146 says the Lord loved the righteous, but the wicked he will bring to
ruin. When we look around us, we may wonder what is taking the Lord
so long. *Hurry up and get to it!* we may think. "Give those wicked their
lump of coal," we may say, "and may it burn along with them in their
well-deserved fiery comeuppance!" Why is it taking Jesus so long to
show up with his two lists and remake the world anew once and for
all? Can't he see the suffering that the wicked have wrought?

In anticipating the destruction of the wicked, we tend to forget
the crucial message of the Gospel: Jesus entered this world not to
condemn it but to save it. It is by God's mercy, not his indifference to
suffering, that Judgment Day has not yet come. God wants a longer
nice list, and to that end, he has called on us to be instruments of his
redemption. As God's church, we are to sing of the Lord's coming and
the salvation he brings to all. Even without the gift of eternal life in

our hands at this moment, we are to sing a song so sweet, so devoid of malice towards any of our men, that our music may grow the hearts of the wicked and turn them towards the Lord. At all times of year, we should be singing with exceedingly great joy of our Savior, and the song should be so beautiful and sincere that grinches have a change of heart and are forever removed from the naughty list.

Prayer for the Week

Merciful God, who sent your messengers the prophets to preach repentance and prepare the way for our salvation: Give us grace to heed their warnings and forsake our sins, that we may greet with joy the coming of Jesus Christ our Redeemer; who lives and reigns with you and the Holy Spirit, one God, now and for ever. Amen.

Reflective Practice

Take 15-20 minutes today to seriously consider whom you have written off in your life. Who is the person you love to complain about and condemn? Perhaps it is a slacking or vindictive co-worker, an overbearing family member, or some person you've never met but whose world views represent all that you detest. Just when you've called to mind all that irritates you about that person, pray for them in a way that genuinely seeks God's mercy on their behalf. Hold them in love like their life—and your own life—depends on it.

THIRD
WEEK

———

[5]*Blessed is he*
WHOSE HELP
is the God of Jacob,
WHOSE HOPE
is in the Lord his God.

PSALM 146:5

of Advent

SUNDAY

Weary of the Season

 OPEN DWELL AND LISTEN TO
Isaiah 35:1-10; Psalm 146:5-10; James 5:7-10; Matthew 11:2-11

"Pessimism is not in being tired of evil but in being tired of good. Despair does not lie in being weary of suffering, but in being weary of joy."

G.K. CHESTERTON

IT IS THE BEGINNING OF THE THIRD WEEK of Advent, and we may already be weary of the "holiday season." Festive decorations have been up for weeks. Canned tunes about snowmen, Santa Claus, and reindeer are losing their charm. Even Handel's *Messiah* may be starting to sound a little stale. If we eat another Christmas cookie, we may toss our cookies. We've already been to fourteen Christmas parties (or we are aware that everyone else has), and the loneliness of the season is beginning to feel unbearable. By the time Christmas Day finally arrives, we are ready to be through with the whole business.

This season of Advent is a gift to us, the *present* that reminds us to be present in our waiting rather than settling for an immediate, cheap substitution of the real thing. Patience can be difficult to master within ourselves, and the temptation is all around us to choose the sugar cookie over waiting for the Bread of Life. Thankfully, Scripture presents us with helpful encouragement. James tells us to look to the prophets to learn how to persevere in patient waiting. Look to the prophet Isaiah, who says it is in the wilderness, not the big box store, where we will find joy. Trust the prophets. We do not want to miss out on true joy in favor of a cheap substitution just because it has fast, free delivery. Joy is nothing short of the profound, awe-filled recognition that all things in this perishing world are being made new. The desert blooms; the deaf hear; sorrow and sighing will flee away. These things are to be done in the Lord's time, and they are worth waiting for.

Advent is the beginning of the church year. We should not feel stale and weary but refreshed and invigorated. Let us seek out the Lord in the quiet places and be refreshed anew so that we, no longer weary, may be prepared to rejoice in all that is to come.

Prayer for the Week

Stir up your power, O Lord, and with great might come among us; and, because we are sorely hindered by our sins, let your bountiful grace and mercy speedily help and deliver us; through Jesus Christ our Lord, to whom, with you and the Holy Spirit, be honor and glory, now and for ever. *Amen.*

Reflective Practice

Take some time to identify three ways you could fast from the sugar-fueled hyperactivity of the "holiday season" and commit to keeping that fast for the remainder of Advent. These can be small sacrifices like not saying "Merry Christmas" or singing Christmas carols before the 25th or larger sacrifices like refraining from feasting during a fasting season. The important thing is not so much the scale of the sacrifices but that they ensure you do not weary of the joy of Christmas before it arrives.

MONDAY

Longing for Joy

 OPEN DWELL AND LISTEN TO
Psalm 42; Isaiah 29:17-24; Acts 5:12-16

"Joy is distinct not only from pleasure in general but even from aesthetic pleasure. It must have the stab, the pang, the inconsolable longing."

C.S. LEWIS

WHAT IS JOY? We recognize the word and see it everywhere, but how many of us can say what it is? We may think of it as a stronger word for happiness, but there is little relationship between the two. Like two work colleagues in separate departments brushing shoulders at a holiday work function, happiness and joy have a casual acquaintance, but they are hardly close.

Happiness is more immediate, temperamental, and often fleeting. It is like a bubbly, sugar-filled drink. It may delight the taste buds initially, but over time, it goes flat, and its saccharine sweetness only leaves us feeling thirstier. There's nothing wrong with happiness, but it cannot provide what the soul ultimately seeks. In contrast, there is joy, which C.S. Lewis compares to a profound longing. He is echoing Psalm 42, which compares the soul's longing to a deer panting for flowing streams: our souls thirst for the living water of God, and nothing else will quench it.

To truly enter into the spirit of the Christmas season, we must embrace the longing of our souls in Advent. To truly experience the joy of the Christmas season, we must seek out the wellspring that satisfies. This requires patience and the willingness to plumb the depths of our faith rather than be happy with a superficial acquaintance with it. "Deep calls to deep," says the psalm. We must follow that longing within us and go deeper: deeper in our prayers, in our reading of God's word, in our sacrificial service to our neighbor. Only then can we embrace our true heart's desire, the joy which has no end.

Prayer for the Week

Stir up your power, O Lord, and with great might come among us; and, because we are sorely hindered by our sins, let your bountiful grace and mercy speedily help and deliver us; through Jesus Christ our Lord, to whom, with you and the Holy Spirit, be honor and glory, now and for ever. *Amen.*

Reflective Practice

Prayerfully consider one or two ways you feel dissatisfied with your life. How might you understand that dissatisfaction not as a lack of some material or temporal thing but as a longing for a deeper relationship with God? Job dissatisfaction could be a longing for more meaningful work directly serving the kingdom of God. Relationship dissatisfaction could be a reflection of a disordered love or a lack of love contrary to the life of rich fellowship to which God is calling you. Pray for wisdom and for God to provide for your true heart's desire.

TUESDAY

It All Adds Up

 OPEN DWELL AND LISTEN TO
Psalm 42; Ezekiel 47:1-12; Jude 1:17-25

"Mathematics is the language in which God has written the universe."

GALILEO GALILEI

THERE ARE A LOT OF NUMBERS IN THE BIBLE. Many of them we see repeated over and over again—numbers like three, four, seven, twelve, forty, and one thousand. On the one hand, numbers are quite practical and finite. They provide precise measurement and orientation. On the other hand, numbers are the backbone of poetry and music, the patterned rhythm that plays throughout Scripture and draws us into a deeper experience of God's word.

God brings Ezekiel to many places and shows him extraordinary things. For instance, God brings Ezekiel to the back door of the temple, leads him around to where water is flowing out of the temple, and then has Ezekiel pass through the water several times. Each time the water is deeper, and the last time it is so deep that Ezekiel cannot pass through it. God is extremely precise, and his account is packed with numbers. The temple's orientation along the four cardinal directions is specified, and Ezekiel is led four times through the water flowing south from the altar. God is the ultimate navigator, and Ezekiel trusts God to provide the orientation. He walks the precise distances, even if God's purpose is not immediately apparent.

We will spend our whole life, from childhood to our dying breath, discerning what God is asking of us and how to understand it. He may take us 1,000 feet in one direction only to send us right back again. As we walk our strange paths through the many phases of life, we have Scripture as a guide. Like the flowing water in Ezekiel, we will pass through these texts multiple times, particularly the four Gospels. Each time we hear them, their depth increases. While the mystery of God's word can never be fully comprehended, we can be absolutely certain of this: God, the author of all, is using all things to draw us into a deeper relationship with him—even numbers.

Prayer for the Week

Stir up your power, O Lord, and with great might come among us; and, because we are sorely hindered by our sins, let your bountiful grace and mercy speedily help and deliver us; through Jesus Christ our Lord, to whom, with you and the Holy Spirit, be honor and glory, now and for ever. *Amen.*

Reflective Practice

Over the course of this week, pick a favorite Bible passage, or even one at random, and read it four times. Take note of new details that stand out to you each time you read it. What connections to your life does it call to mind that cause you to see those experiences in a new light? If you've read this passage in other periods of your life, how has your understanding of it deepened over time? Finish the week with a prayer of thanksgiving for the gift of God's word and its inexhaustible wisdom.

WEDNESDAY

Clean House

 OPEN DWELL AND LISTEN TO
Psalm 42; Zechariah 8:1-17; Matthew 8:14-17, 28-34

---

*"Rarely do we reflect upon what gifts our souls may possess, who
dwells within them, or how extremely precious they are. Therefore,
we do little to preserve their beauty; all our care is concentrated
on our bodies, which are but the coarse setting of the diamond, or
the outer walls of the castle."*

ST. TERESA OF ÁVILA

WE PAY CONSIDERABLE ATTENTION TO what we put into our
bodies. Food labels make statements like no high fructose corn syrup,
no artificial colors, no GMOs, no parabens, cage-free, organic, and the
list goes on. Caring for our bodies certainly is a good thing: imperfect
and fragile as bodies are, they are a gift from God. Indeed, God the
Son came down from heaven and was born into a body just like ours,
and that same body was resurrected from the dead, further affirming
its goodness.

It can be more of a challenge to care for our souls. We can't see them or
touch them, and the packaging of the world doesn't cater to keeping
them in good condition. Yet, care for our bodies is pointless without
equal or even greater attention paid to the well-being of our souls. To
better care for the soul, it can be helpful to have a way to think about
what the soul is. St. Teresa of Ávila envisions the soul as a beautiful
mansion or castle in which God reigns at the center. It is a lovely
image, but imagine what happens to a castle, or any home, when it is
neglected. Cracks appear in the walls, moisture collects, mold grows,

vermin build nests, and soon, this once beautiful home becomes a place with which you want less and less to do. The neglect deepens, and then, possibly without our realizing it, squatters have taken up residence.

Throughout the Gospels, we hear a great deal about Jesus casting out demons. They possess a body, but their headquarters are the soul. By allowing vices like anger to fester, gluttony to rot, greed to seep, and lust to burn, the soul deteriorates, and demons are the squatters that move in. Through diligent prayer, the practice of virtue, and the habitual confession of our sins, we can clear out the mess, dirt, and decay in our souls and make it a place not fit for the Prince of Darkness but for the Prince of Peace.

Prayer for the Week

Stir up your power, O Lord, and with great might come among us; and, because we are sorely hindered by our sins, let your bountiful grace and mercy speedily help and deliver us; through Jesus Christ our Lord, to whom, with you and the Holy Spirit, be honor and glory, now and for ever. *Amen.*

Reflective Practice

Most churches provide well-considered words for confessing our sins. Look up one of these confessions and read it slowly aloud, allowing the meaning of the words to sink in and resonate. Prayerfully consider how these words shine a light on the dark places in your own soul. Identify one small dark corner and pray about how you, through God's help and mercy, can go about repairing the damage and decay that this sin has wrought.

THURSDAY

Are You Listening?

 OPEN DWELL AND LISTEN TO

Psalm 80:1-7, 17-19; 2 Samuel 7:1-17; Galatians 3:23-29

"I have often regretted the words I have spoken, but I have never regretted my silence."

ABBA ARSENIUS THE GREAT

GOD IS ALWAYS SPEAKING AND MOVING towards us in love. Never is there a moment in which his presence is absent from our world. In fact, this is one of the central truths and promises of Advent: God draws near to us in the person of Jesus Christ as an embodiment of his eternal love. Yet to reflect on his merciful love is, in the same breath, to be reminded of our own wayward inattentiveness. He speaks, yet do we listen?

Listening is remarkably difficult, for it requires of us an ability to silence our own thoughts and opinions, as well as the perceived need to share those with others. To listen is to open one's heart to the insights and wisdom of another. As we do, especially in our relationship with God, we are reminded that he is the ultimate source of wisdom, our Father whose words we do well to hear and obey.

Time and time again, our relationship to God in Scripture is described in familial terms. As 2 Samuel 7:14 says, "I will be to him a father, and he shall be to me a son." At its very best, the parent/child relationship is defined by the gift of time. A parent is present to their child, emotionally and physically, offering constant guidance and encouragement in the way of truth. Yet how many times do parents have to remind their children to listen? Kids, young and old alike, struggle to willingly receive the wisdom and direction of their parents.

This struggle is true of our earthly relationships and reflects our ongoing life with God. He is a perfect Father to us, yet we are either too busy with other passions and pursuits or struggle to fully trust that his word is true and for our good. However, in the midst of our busyness and doubts, Advent is an invitation to silence our mouths and hearts, for even a moment, to hear again the eternal words of wisdom from our faithful Father.

Prayer for the Week

Stir up your power, O Lord, and with great might come among us; and, because we are sorely hindered by our sins, let your bountiful grace and mercy speedily help and deliver us; through Jesus Christ our Lord, to whom, with you and the Holy Spirit, be honor and glory, now and for ever. *Amen.*

Reflective Practice

Be mindful today of how you use your words. Are you quick to speak and slow to listen? Cultivate a practice of intentional silence today, uncomfortable as it may be, so that you can tune your heart to hear afresh the quiet voice of our Lord.

FRIDAY

Rescue and Return

 OPEN DWELL AND LISTEN TO
Psalm 80:1-7, 17-19; 2 Samuel 7:18-22; Galatians 4:1-7

"Hush your tongue that your heart may speak, and hush your heart that God may speak."

ST. JOHN OF DALYATHA

SALVATION LIES AT THE VERY HEART of the Christian message. We "get saved" at church or summer camp. We often set out on evangelistic missions to "save the world." We pray for the salvation of friends or family members. Yet rarely do we pause and ask a more fundamental question: saved from what?

Especially in a modern world that enjoys unparalleled levels of affluence and health, this message of salvation to many may feel like a relic from a bygone era. And tempting as this utopian vision may be, the myth of progress is shattered in each and every generation, for the sickness of sin is an unavoidable virus that corrupts even the most advanced societies. Salvation is as timely and needed as ever.

The psalmist in today's reading cries out for salvation, giving voice to the deepest cry of the human heart: "Restore us, O God; let your face shine, that we may be saved!" (Ps 80:3).

Humanity's deepest sickness is an alienation from God that leads to death. It is the eternal loneliness and isolation of people who once knew the Source of all that is good and life-giving, yet freely turned their backs on it, searching instead for their own self-fulfilling destiny.

This is the sickness of our first ancestors, and it is the pervasive ailment that infects each one of us.

As such, salvation is both a rescue and a return. We are rescued from ourselves and returned to the gift of community, knowing and being known as we enter the dance of the Trinity. In fact, we can only know ourselves when the light of God's countenance shines on us. And though he longs to be known, he does not force himself on us, instead patiently waiting for us to call on him from the deepest parts of our souls.

Prayer for the Week

Stir up your power, O Lord, and with great might come among us; and, because we are sorely hindered by our sins, let your bountiful grace and mercy speedily help and deliver us; through Jesus Christ our Lord, to whom, with you and the Holy Spirit, be honor and glory, now and for ever. *Amen.*

Reflective Practice

Take time today to reflect on the reality of sin as isolation. Can you identify areas of your life that are cut off from streams of life and the gift of communion with God and others? Are there simple steps to move away from this loneliness and into the warmth of community?

SATURDAY

Believe and Obey

 OPEN DWELL AND LISTEN TO

Psalm 80:1-7, 17-19; 2 Samuel 7:23-29; John 3:31-36

"Christians, instead of arming themselves with swords, extend their hands in prayer."

ST. ATHANASIUS THE GREAT

BELIEVE AND OBEY. This invitation found in John 3 is truly an entry into the way of life for each generation: belief in Christ that leads to a life of obedience and obedience animated by the abiding life of the Spirit. The two support and shape each other and, when isolated from one another, can lead well-meaning followers of Jesus down many a wayward path.

As the Scriptures remind us elsewhere, belief in Christ in and of itself is not a sufficient guide to the way of life (Jas 2:19). Of course, belief in Christ is vitally important, and Advent focuses our hearts and minds on a set of beliefs: namely, the historic incarnation of Jesus Christ for the life of the world. Still, one can know of this event, and even believe it to be true, yet go along living as though it has no impact upon them or their world. The Prince of Peace may have come, yet we can choose to persist in lives defined by violence, power, and greed.

What is required is a radical transformation of life, a belief *that leads to obedience.*

Similarly, blind obedience and acceptance of an abstracted list of moral standards is *not* the fullness of life for which Christ came.

While faithfulness to the commands of Christ should be central to the life of every believer, our obedience to his ways is meant to train us in the way that is good, teaching us to long for his presence and abide with him through prayer. *This* is why we believe and obey, for it is the very path to his presence, a life of communion with God.

Prayer for the Week

Stir up your power, O Lord, and with great might come among us; and, because we are sorely hindered by our sins, let your bountiful grace and mercy speedily help and deliver us; through Jesus Christ our Lord, to whom, with you and the Holy Spirit, be honor and glory, now and for ever. *Amen.*

Reflective Practice

In your own life, what is the relationship between belief in Christ and obedience to his ways? Are they close companions and intimate friends, or does one seem to overpower the other and lead to an imbalance in your life of discipleship?

FOURTH
WEEK

———

³Restore us, O God;

LET YOUR

FACE SHINE,

that we may be saved!

PSALM 80:3

of Advent

SUNDAY

Healing Medicine

 OPEN DWELL AND LISTEN TO
Isaiah 7:10-16; Psalm 80:1-7, 17-19; Romans 1:1-7; Matthew 1:18-25

"Today we received a gift which we did not ask for; let us bestow alms to those who cry out to us and beg!"

ST. EPHRAIM THE SYRIAN

HAVE YOU EVER BEEN SO SICK that you found yourself unable to do anything that might help or improve your condition? Mercifully, for most of us, these moments are few and far between. Yet even the healthiest among us have had an unwelcome virus take over and wreak havoc on our bodies. A simple sip of water required unthinkable strength; we were too weak to call out to a caretaker and ask for the medicine that would bring much-needed healing. The sickness simply won control of every part of us, and we were at its mercy.

Though we often push it to the side and try to ignore the symptoms, this severe illness is the truest diagnosis of the human condition apart from God.

The sickness of sin runs so deep and infects us so thoroughly that we lack the strength to seek healing and wholeness. We may know there is a hospital for our souls, yet we're too weak to check ourselves in. We are weak and weary people, yet in the words of Isaiah, even though we cannot cry out to him, the Lord himself comes and finds us, giving us a sign of hope. "Behold, the virgin shall conceive and bear a son, and shall call his name Immanuel" (Isa 7:14).

The presence of God with us in Christ is the healing medicine we were too weak to seek out, the gift for which we didn't even know we could ask. And so, we receive it in our weakness, share it joyfully with others, and believe it to be for our health and the salvation of our souls and bodies.

Prayer for the Week

Purify our conscience, Almighty God, by your daily visitation, that your Son Jesus Christ, at his coming, may find in us a mansion prepared for himself; who lives and reigns with you, in the unity of the Holy Spirit, one God, now and for ever. *Amen.*

Reflective Practice

Just as Christ drew near to you in your sin and sickness when you didn't expect it and couldn't ask for it, how can you do the same for others, offering the gift of God's mercy and love in word and deed to those who might least expect it?

MONDAY

Anguish

OPEN DWELL AND LISTEN TO

1 Samuel 2:1-10; Genesis 17:15-22; Galatians 4:8-20

"As the human race fell into bondage to death by means of a virgin, so it is rescued by a virgin."

ST. IRENAEUS OF LYONS

CHILDBIRTH, TO BORROW A WORD FROM ST. PAUL, IS "ANGUISH" (Gal 4:18). Of course, this was not an anguish that he knew firsthand. Yet, as any mother can tell you, few pains compare to the intense suffering of bringing a child into this world, not to mention the months of discomfort and sacrifice that precede the birth itself. And yet, quite remarkably, this is an anguish that countless women willingly take upon themselves! Why? Because they have set their hearts on the joy and wonder of parenthood and know *that* is what will endure. The pain of birth recedes into the background.

During the Advent season, we remember the Mother of our Lord, Mary, as a perfect example of sacrificial motherhood. She not only willingly took upon herself the anguish of childbirth but also received the prophetic words spoken over her with joy. Through her surrender to the will of God, the life of God was born into the world. As she marveled at her son speaking with authority in the Temple, the message of God's rescue mission was boldly proclaimed. And as she wept at the cross of her beloved son, death was there destroyed, once and for all, opening to us the way of life.

In the moment when our pain or sorrow is endured in isolation, it can feel profoundly confusing, overwhelming, and disorienting. Yet, could it be that this pain, which feels like death, is in fact giving way to birth, to the very life of Christ being formed in us? (Gal 4:19). Let us lift our eyes toward the heavenly kingdom of God and choose to believe that every anguish in this life will be healed by the infinite mercy of God.

Prayer for the Week

Purify our conscience, Almighty God, by your daily visitation, that your Son Jesus Christ, at his coming, may find in us a mansion prepared for himself; who lives and reigns with you, in the unity of the Holy Spirit, one God, now and for ever. *Amen.*

Reflective Practice

What pain, sorrow, or even anguish are you facing that can be reframed in light of God's great story of redemption? Take time today to reflect on this question. In prayer, ask the Lord to deepen his life within you in and through this momentary trial.

TUESDAY

Humbled by the Mystery

 OPEN DWELL AND LISTEN TO

1 Samuel 2:1-10; Genesis 21:1-21; Galatians 4:21-5:1

"In the things of God, the confession of no knowledge is great knowledge."

ST. CYRIL OF JERUSALEM

AS CHRISTMAS DAY DRAWS EVER CLOSER, our Advent journey has been nothing short of a biblical and theological feast. We have walked through some of the most significant passages in the Old and New Testaments, reflecting on how each points to Christ and finds its fulfillment in him. And, as wonderful as this season of thoughtful reflection undoubtedly is, we must remember today that the aim of this season is not simply expanded knowledge but a lived encounter with the living God.

Advent is not a problem to solve or a code to crack. It is a mystery to encounter and a wonder meant to captivate us to the core. So, after many days of reflective words and expanded knowledge, we are invited to be still. Let us reflect on the words of 1 Samuel, where we are told, "Talk no more so very proudly, let not arrogance come from your mouth; for the Lord is a God of knowledge, and by him actions are weighed (1 Sam 2:3).

What can we truly "understand" of the Word of God made flesh? Who in their wildest imagination could have ever dreamed of such an audacious story of redemption? How can the created give voice to the will and mind of the creator?

God is with us: of this there is no doubt. Let us resist the urge to analyze or measure the mystery and, instead, await his birth with reverent awe and gratitude.

Prayer for the Week

Purify our conscience, Almighty God, by your daily visitation, that your Son Jesus Christ, at his coming, may find in us a mansion prepared for himself; who lives and reigns with you, in the unity of the Holy Spirit, one God, now and for ever. *Amen*.

Reflective Practice

Take a walk outside and leave your phone behind. Consider praying a portion of this week's prayer as a "breath prayer," repeating it meditatively as you breathe in and out. "Purify my conscience, Almighty God, by your daily visitation," or "When you come, may you find a mansion prepared for yourself."

WEDNESDAY

Generation
to Generation

 OPEN DWELL AND LISTEN TO

1 Samuel 2:1-10; Genesis 37:2-11; Matthew 1:1-17

"Fire and water do not mix, neither can you mix judgment of others with the desire to repent."

ST. JOHN CLIMACUS

IN TODAY'S PASSAGES FROM GENESIS AND MATTHEW, you may have noticed a shared theme and common focus. Both speak of generations and genealogies, tracing the story of God's faithfulness to a specific family over many centuries. In what may seem like nothing more than a running list of names, one discovers the very hopes and dreams of people who lived and longed, hoped and feared, just like we do today.

If you were to look at the names on your own family tree, especially the ones known to you personally, you would immediately realize there's so much more to a genealogy than a simple list of biological connections. Some names may bring forth emotions of great warmth and affection as you remember moments of tenderness and selfless love. On the other hand, the name of someone who brought great shame or scandal to your family's story may bring a wave of anger and bitterness crashing over you.

This is the reality of living within a family. It is messy and frail, a source of both belonging and alienation. And it is into the chaos of the human familial experience that our Lord was born, taking this family story as his own, not shying away from past failures but drawing it all unto himself to heal it and make it whole. This was true for Christ's immediate ancestors, and it is also true for the entire human race—and for your own story.

In the birth of Jesus, the past is redeemed and the future secured. We can look back, not with judgment or bitterness towards others, but with sorrow for our *own* sins and the part we may have played in our family's story of brokenness. And as we do, we learn to walk in newness of life, trusting solely in the mercy and peace of God.

Prayer for the Week

Purify our conscience, Almighty God, by your daily visitation, that your Son Jesus Christ, at his coming, may find in us a mansion prepared for himself; who lives and reigns with you, in the unity of the Holy Spirit, one God, now and for ever. *Amen.*

Reflective Practice

Reproduce the most thorough family tree you're able to draw from memory. What emotions surface within you as you do? Are there names that shine a light on old wounds? People whose investment in you made you who you are today? Take time in prayer to give thanks for all things, the good and the bad, believing every part of your story is held secure by the Lord.

Days Around

CHRISTMAS
DAY
—

7ASCRIBE TO THE
LORD, *O families of*
the peoples, ascribe to the Lord
glory and strength!

PSALM 96:7

DECEMBER 22

All Generations

 OPEN DWELL AND LISTEN TO

Luke 1:46b-55; Isaiah 33:17-22; Revelation 22:6-7, 18-20

"The Babe that I carry carries me, says Mary."

ST. EPHRAIM THE SYRIAN

IN LUKE'S GOSPEL, AS MARY ECHOES Hannah's Song from 1 Samuel, we find a remarkable phrase in the Magnificat: "From now on all generations will call me blessed" (Luke 1:48). Having just received the divine word from on high, has Mary now let this announcement go to her head? For our modern ears, it is difficult to imagine anyone saying something as bold as "all generations" will remember and bless their name. Yet I wonder, might our confusion at Mary's claim reveal our own failure to grasp the unique and unrepeatable nature of her part in the story of salvation?

Only one human in history has given birth to the uncreated God. Mary carried within her body the very one that sustained her every breath. Through her humility and openness to the miraculous work of God in and through her, healing and hope entered the world. So, when she speaks of her blessedness throughout the generations, it is not *herself* or her own faithfulness that she is elevating. She is instead marveling at the mercy of God and *his* unspeakable goodness on display through her.

For us to retain a faithful perspective on Mary as the first disciple and mother of all Christians, we must never separate her from her son. The reverence given to her in Scripture and throughout the history of the Church is inseparably connected to the babe within her womb. When we reflect on Mary's story, especially in the Advent season, it is always meant to point us to Christ and invite us to model the same response of faithfulness and humility, saying to the Lord, "Let it be to me according to your word" (Luke 1:38).

Prayer for the Week

Purify our conscience, Almighty God, by your daily visitation, that your Son Jesus Christ, at his coming, may find in us a mansion prepared for himself; who lives and reigns with you, in the unity of the Holy Spirit, one God, now and for ever. *Amen.*

Reflective Practice

Take time to re-read Mary's Magnificat today, giving thanks to God for her faithful witness. Pray for the strength to respond with a similar faith in your own life, believing that the life of God can be nurtured and grown within you.

DECEMBER 23

Who Am I?

 OPEN DWELL AND LISTEN TO

Luke 1:46b-55; 2 Samuel 7:18, 23-29; Galatians 3:6-14

"You should continually and unceasingly call to mind all the blessings which God in His love has bestowed on you in the past, and still bestows for the salvation of your soul."

ST. MARK THE ASCETIC

THROUGHOUT SCRIPTURE, ONE FINDS MOMENTS of great humility when the chasm between creature and creator is acutely felt. And perhaps nowhere greater is this seen than in the heartfelt prayers of King David. As he says in the Psalms, "What is man that you are mindful of him?" (Ps 8:4). Or, as we see in today's passage, he goes before the Lord and says, "Who am I, O Lord God, and what is my house, that you have brought me thus far?" (2 Sam 7:18).

David was a flawed man, at times overcome by his distorted passions and desires, yet also defined by his longing to know God and be known by him. And when he came to his senses and saw how his decisions led to his own self-made isolation, he wept bitterly over his sins and pleaded for the Lord's healing touch. In short, he was a human being, imperfect yet loved by God and transformed by that love. In one way or another, David is infinitely relatable: each of us finds our own stories within his life and prayers.

Living with an awareness of our sin and God's mercy leads us to a life of profound gratitude. We know the gap between our brokenness and God's holiness, and yet our Lord continually draws near, never finding a distance he cannot cross to reach those he loves. This, of course, is the message of Advent and the hope of Christmas. Though our sin and sickness have led us astray and taken us off course, God comes to us in Christ, entering the chaos and confusion to bring us back to him.

Prayer for the Week

Purify our conscience, Almighty God, by your daily visitation, that your Son Jesus Christ, at his coming, may find in us a mansion prepared for himself; who lives and reigns with you, in the unity of the Holy Spirit, one God, now and for ever. *Amen.*

Reflective Practice

Take time today to intentionally cultivate a spirit of gratitude in your heart and life. Identify specific events, circumstances, relationships, or sources of provision for which you can express gratitude to God in an intentional moment of thanksgiving and praise.

DECEMBER 24

Center Stage

 OPEN DWELL AND LISTEN TO

Isaiah 9:2-7; Psalm 96; Titus 2:11-14; Luke 2:1-14

"This Nativity night bestowed peace on the whole world;
So let no one threaten;
This is the night of the Most Gentle One — let no one be cruel;
This is the night of the Humble One — let no one be proud.
Today the Divine Being took upon Himself the seal of our humanity,
In order for humanity to be decorated by the Seal of Divinity."

ST. ISAAC THE SYRIAN

AN EMPIRE IS NO SMALL THING TO WIN. Fortunately, the emperor
has thousands of ministers to help him keep it safe. He calls for a
global census, and the great machine springs to life: paper shuffling,
fact-checking, fees changing hands, soldiers patrolling. This is the
most organized, the most supreme rule the world has known. It has
done much real good. And it has brought peace—of a kind. This is the
Pax Romana, the Roman Peace, formidable and useful.

But who are those crucified by the side of the road? Pay no heed. There
is peace for those who say "Caesar is lord" and forget what must
sometimes happen to make him so.

Is this the peace of God's people? Is this the "desire of the nations"?

In Isaiah, we hear of an army. They've come back from war, boots and
fatigues stained—with conquering, peacekeeping, or a combination
of both. A fire is lit. Every uniform goes into the fire and is burned up

forever. And then a baby is born, of little account. He is one small name on the empire's list. Angels appear, dressed in blazing light, to announce his coming. They're a myriad, a "host"—in Greek, an "army."

In the Gospel of Luke, it is difficult to avoid the sense that something more real is going on behind the scenes of merely human power. What seems most worth preserving is giving way; a whole new way is breaking through.

Will we catch the prophet's vision? As real as it seems, earthly power has been, all this time, an opening act at best, a stand-in. The scene has just changed. The Virgin Mary and Joseph have prepared backstage, the angels have opened the curtain, and now this infant, put in place by God's power, has quietly taken center stage. He will take the lead.

A child conquers nothing. He enforces nothing. And yet, he is surrounded by angel armies. He will come into his own. He will carry his own cross and judge all powers by his sacrifice.

Prayer for Christmas Eve

O God, you have caused this holy night to shine with the brightness of the true Light: Grant that we, who have known the mystery of that Light on earth, may also enjoy him perfectly in heaven; where with you and the Holy Spirit he lives and reigns, one God, in glory everlasting. *Amen.*

Reflective Practice

Still yourself. Say aloud, slowly, for up to 10 minutes, Unto you is born this day in the city of David a savior. If you believe this to be true, how might you live with less anxiety and greater security today? Ask the Lord for peace, not of the emperor but of the Infant.

Christmas Day

⁶The HEAVENS
PROCLAIM *his*
righteousness, and all
the peoples SEE
HIS GLORY.

PSALM 97:6

DECEMBER 25

Say Yes to the Call

 OPEN DWELL AND LISTEN TO

Isaiah 62:6-12; Psalm 97; Titus 3:4-7; Luke 2:8-20

"I know God will not give me anything I can't handle. I just wish that He didn't trust me so much."

ST. TERESA OF CALCUTTA (MOTHER TERESA)

THE VIRGIN MARY, THE MOTHER OF JESUS, is often contrasted with Eve. Persuaded by the devil, Eve chose to ignore what God had asked of her, believing she knew better. Conversely, when the archangel Gabriel came to the Virgin and told her she would be the mother of God, she said, "Be it unto me according to thy will." In other words, Eve said no to God; Mary said yes.

Saying yes to God is no easy thing. As we see throughout Scripture and in the lives of the saints, God does not make small demands of his servants. Honestly, it can be difficult to walk that road of faith without stumbling. Sure, we may feel great saying yes to God initially, but then the road drags on over months or even years. The road that at first seemed bright and full of exciting promise can grow rocky, dark, and long. Put another way, saying yes to God can initially feel like Christmas morning—all bright and hopeful—but now it's the middle of February, and that Christmas feeling is long gone. Now everything just feels dark, cold, and more than a little depressing.

In such times in our life, between Christmas and spring, we may begin to wonder whether saying yes to God was a huge mistake. In such times, we can be encouraged by the Virgin Mary's example.

Her road took her from the first Christmas, with angels singing on high, to cradling the body of her dead son at Calvary. Yet, despite the dark place her path took her, she continued to trust, without any real-world guarantee, that God had all things in hand. With each bend in her road, no matter how rocky or dark the terrain got, Mary continued to say yes to God. Ultimately, that yes took her—and all of us—to the door of an empty tomb. On this glorious Christmas Day, let us commit to saying yes to God's demands on our life and follow that road, as Mary did, trusting that he has all things in hand.

Prayer for Christmas Day

Almighty God, you have given your only-begotten Son to take our nature upon him, and to be born this day of a pure virgin: Grant that we, who have been born again and made your children by adoption and grace, may daily be renewed by your Holy Spirit; through our Lord Jesus Christ, to whom with you and the same Spirit be honor and glory, now and for ever. *Amen.*

Reflective Practice

Consider the demands God has made on your own life. Whom has God called you to serve? Who are the least of God's people whose lives bump up against your own? Prayerfully consider how you might answer the call to better serve and love your neighbor, always remembering that when we serve the least of God's children, we are serving the one we celebrate this day and all days. A blessed Christmas to you!

End Notes

NOTES:

NOTES:

Made in the USA
Coppell, TX
10 November 2022